The Royal Family

HARRY
~ and ~
# MEGHAN

IZZI HOWELL

PowerKiDS
press

Published in 2020 by The Rosen Publishing Group, Inc.
29 East 21st Street, New York, NY 10010

Cataloging-in-Publication Data

Names: Howell, Izzi.
Title: Harry and Meghan / Izzi Howell.
Description: New York : PowerKids Press, 2020. | Series: The royal family | Includes glossary and index.
Identifiers: ISBN 9781725303935 (pbk.) | ISBN 9781725303959 (library bound) | ISBN 9781725303942 (6pack)
Subjects: LCSH: Harry, Prince, Duke of Sussex, 1984–Juvenile literature. | Meghan, Duchess of Sussex, 1981–Juvenile literature. | Royal couples–Great Britain–Biography–Juvenile literature.
Classification: LCC DA591.A45 H68 2020 | DDC 941.086092'2 B–dc23

Editor: Izzi Howell
Designer: Clare Nicholas
In-house editor: Amy Pimperton

Picture acknowledgements:
Alamy: dpa picture alliance 25; Getty: Karwai Tang/WireImage cover and 4, Max Mumby/Indigo 5, kylieellway 6, Anwar Hussein 7t, Samir Hussein/WireImage 7b, 17c and 17b, Julian Parker/UK Press 8, Tim Graham Picture Library 9, George Marks 11t, stevegeer 11b, JOHN STILLWELL/AFP 12b, MyImages_Micha 13t, CLINT HUGHES/AFP 13b, audioundwerbung 14, Ian Watson/USA Network/NBCU Photo Bank 15t, Kanoke_46 16, Owen Humphreys - WPA Pool 18, BEN STANSALL/AFP 19, STEVE PARSONS/AFP 21, Anatoliy Cherkasov/NurPhoto 23, Sylvain Gaboury/Patrick McMullan 24, DMC/GC Images 27; Royal Navy: Crown Copyright (2012), PO Terry Seward 12t; Shutterstock: Ingus Kruklitis 10, Papuchalka – kaelaimages 15b, Hadrian 20 and 29, JONATHAN PLEDGER 22, Ivan Mateev 26t, Svetography 26b, LINGTREN IMAGES 31.
All graphic elements courtesy of Shutterstock.

Manufactured in the United States of America

CPSIA Compliance Information: Batch CSPK19: For Further Information contact Rosen Publishing, New York, New York at 1-800-237-9932.

CONTENTS

Harry and Meghan

— • • • —

On May 19, 2018, Meghan Markle married Prince Harry and became an official member of the British royal family. Meghan and Harry are ambassadors for the UK at home and overseas. They are invited to meet people and attend events to improve relationships between different countries.

The royal couple

Prince Harry is the grandson of Queen Elizabeth II. He is sixth in line to the throne, after his father, brother William, and William's children. His wife, Meghan, was born in the United States, but is now a British citizen. They hold the titles of the Duke and Duchess of Sussex.

Royal duties

As members of the royal family, Harry and Meghan spend much of their time carrying out official duties. They visit schools and hospitals and attend events and ceremonies to show their support. Sometimes, they meet important leaders from other countries when they visit the UK.

Meghan and Harry meet a young fan after attending the Commonwealth church service in March 2018.

∨

HARRY AND MEGHAN FUN FACTS

Harry trekked to the South Pole in 2013 with a team of injured soldiers.

Meghan is a close friend of the tennis player Serena Williams.

Harry thinks that some children are disappointed when they meet him, as they expect the prince to wear a cape or a crown!

Meghan launched her own fashion line in 2016.

Around the world

Travel is an important part of Harry and Meghan's royal responsibilities. When the royal family makes an official visit to another country, they meet people who live there and learn about the country's traditions and culture. The royal family often visits Commonwealth countries, and countries where the Queen is the Head of State, to maintain a good relationship between them and the UK.

Harry's Royal Family

Harry's grandparents, father, and brother are all members of the British royal family.

The Queen and Prince Philip arrive at the Trooping the Colour ceremony in 2015. >

Grandparents

Queen Elizabeth II is Harry's grandmother. As Queen, she is the Head of State and Head of the Church of England. She is responsible for entertaining foreign leaders at meals and parties. Every year, the Queen leads the ceremony to open Parliament and attends state events, such as Trooping the Colour. Prince Philip, the Queen's husband, used to help her with these duties, but he is now retired.

Parents

Harry is the son of Prince Charles and Diana Spencer. Charles and Diana's relationship was quite unhappy. They eventually got divorced in 1996. Diana was killed in a car crash in 1997, when Harry was only 12 years old. It was very hard for Harry to lose his mother at such a young age. In 2015, Charles remarried. His second wife, Camilla, Duchess of Cornwall, is Harry's stepmother.

∧ Harry walked behind the coffin with his brother, father, grandfather, and uncle during Diana's funeral.

William and Kate

Harry has always been close to his brother, Prince William. Harry is also good friends with William's wife, Kate, and thinks of her as "the sister he never had." Harry loves playing with William and Kate's three children – Prince George, Princess Charlotte, and Prince Louis.

ROYAL TALK

"Ever since our mother died, obviously we were close, but he is the one person on this earth who I can actually really, you know, we can talk about anything."

Prince Harry spoke about his relationship with Prince William in an interview in 2005.

< Harry, William, and Kate take part in a race during a training day for people running the London Marathon in support of their mental health charity, Heads Together, in 2017.

The Young Prince

Prince Henry Charles Albert David was born on September 15, 1984, at St. Mary's Hospital, London. Crowds of people stood outside the hospital, waiting for news of his birth.

City and countryside

When Harry was a child, his parents lived quite separate lives in different houses. Harry went back and forth between them, enjoying different activities with Charles and Diana. When he was with Diana in London, they would go to the zoo and the movies and eat burgers at fast-food restaurants. When he was with Charles at his countryside home, Harry enjoyed riding ponies and exploring nature.

< Harry and Diana slide down a water ride at the Thorpe Park theme park in 1992.

Harry had a pet rabbit when he was a child. He grew carrots in Charles's vegetable garden to feed to the rabbit!

Off to school

Harry went to nursery school and primary school in London. At the age of eight, Harry started at the same boarding school as his brother, William. The boys lived and studied at school, coming home to see their family on weekends and for holidays. Harry slept in a dormitory with four other boys.

An Eton education

In 1998, Harry went to Eton College. He sometimes found his lessons difficult, but he was excellent at sports. He played on the school's rugby, cricket, and polo teams. In 2003, he left Eton with grades good enough to allow him to join the army. Before he started his training, Harry took a gap year. He worked on a cattle farm in Australia and made a documentary about orphaned children in Lesotho, Africa.

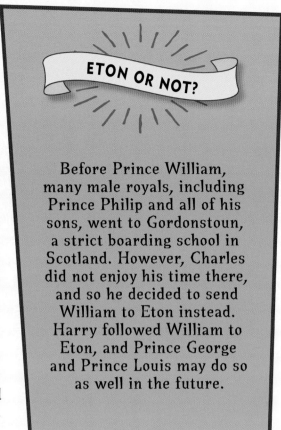

ETON OR NOT?

Before Prince William, many male royals, including Prince Philip and all of his sons, went to Gordonstoun, a strict boarding school in Scotland. However, Charles did not enjoy his time there, and so he decided to send William to Eton instead. Harry followed William to Eton, and Prince George and Prince Louis may do so as well in the future.

∨ Harry enjoyed painting and studying art at Eton College.

Growing Up

••• •••

Rachel Meghan Markle was born on August 4, 1981, in Los Angeles, California. Her parents, Thomas Markle and Doria Ragland, chose to call their daughter by her middle name – Meghan.

Meghan Markle is the first mixed-race member of the British royal family. Her father is white and her mother is African American.

A Hollywood childhood

Meghan grew up in Hollywood with her parents. Thomas was a lighting designer on successful TV shows, while Doria worked as a social worker and taught yoga. At the age of six, Meghan's parents divorced and she went to live with her mother. Meghan visited her father after school on the TV filming set where he worked. It was there that Meghan got her first glimpses of the world of television.

∨ As a child, Meghan lived in the famous Hollywood area of Los Angeles, California, where many films and TV shows are made.

ROYAL TALK

"When you saw Meg on stage, even as a kid, it was clear she was going to be a star."

Meghan's half brother, Tom Jr., from her father's first marriage, talks about his sister in an interview in 2017.

Fighting for what's right

Meghan was passionate about speaking out against injustice from a young age. At the age of 11, she started a campaign to change an advertisement for dish soap that was only aimed at women. Meghan believed that the ad was sexist, making it sound as if only women should be doing the dishes. So, she sent letters to lawyers and kids' news TV programs to raise awareness. They all supported her campaign and the tagline was changed within a few months.

As a child, Meghan spoke up about sexist ads that suggested that only women do housework.

>

Moving on

After high school, Meghan moved to Chicago, Illinois, to study theater and international relations at Northwestern University. This degree combined two of her main interests – acting and global issues. While she was at the university, Meghan also had the opportunity to travel. In 2003, she did an internship at the US embassy in Buenos Aires, Argentina, where she got to see global politics in action.

Northwestern University, Chicago
∨

Army Days

After college, Harry followed family and royal tradition and joined the armed forces. He served in the army for ten years, during which he carried out two tours of active service in Afghanistan.

Into battle

Harry began his army training in 2005. He went through a tough 44-week course, living alongside other army recruits. In 2006, Harry's unit went to serve on the front line in Iraq. Harry did not go with them, as people were worried that he would be a target, making it more dangerous for everyone in his unit. The following year, Harry served for ten weeks in secret in Afghanistan. He patrolled dangerous areas and helped other soldiers fight off enemy attacks.

ROYALS IN WAR ZONES

Harry is not the first royal to serve in a war zone. His uncle, Prince Andrew, worked as a helicopter pilot during the Falklands War in 1982. However, serving in war zones is considered too risky for royals who are likely to become king, such as William.

< Harry takes a break with the other soldiers while serving in Afghanistan in 2007.

Flying high

When Harry came back from Afghanistan, he was chosen to train as an Apache helicopter pilot. This is one of the most difficult roles in the military. A lot of skill is needed to fly Apache helicopters and control their weapons. In September 2012, Harry returned to active service in Afghanistan. He flew an Apache helicopter in combat and helped to evacuate injured soldiers.

∧ Two pilots are needed to fly an Apache helicopter.

As a prince, Harry does not use a last name. In the army, he was known as Officer, and later Captain, Wales instead. This is because his father, Charles, is the Prince of Wales.

Supporting soldiers

In 2014, Harry left active service and started organizing military events that celebrated and commemorated people who served in the armed forces. Later, he also worked on projects that supported injured servicemen and women. Harry officially left the army in 2015, but he is still passionate about supporting the armed forces.

Harry meets soldiers from the the Queen's Own Yeomanry unit in Wigan, UK, in 2016.
∨

Becoming an Actor

— • •• • —

Meghan had always had a passion for drama, and so making a living from acting was an obvious choice. However, it took determination and patience for her to achieve the acting success that she has today.

First roles

Meghan started her acting career before leaving college. In 2002, she appeared on TV screens for the first time on an episode of a medical drama called *General Hospital*. However, she found it hard to find work as an actress after graduation. She managed to find some acting work in small roles on TV shows, and eventually movies.

Meghan was comfortable working on a film set because she had spent so much time on set with her father as a child. ∨

MEGHAN'S FIRST MARRIAGE

In 2004, Meghan started a relationship with Trevor Engelson. They both worked in the film industry — Meghan as an actor and Trevor as a producer. The couple got married in Jamaica in 2011, but divorced two years later in 2013.

In the show *Suits*, Meghan's character Rachel trains to become a lawyer and later works as one.

A starring role

Meghan's big break came in 2011, when she got the main part of Rachel Zane in the TV series *Suits*. The show is about a team of lawyers who work in New York City. Meghan left her job on *Suits* after she married Harry, as she is no longer working as an actor.

Making money

In between acting roles, Meghan earned a living through other jobs. She worked as a calligrapher, creating beautiful handwritten letters for clients. She also started her own lifestyle website called *The Tig*. Meghan's website had articles on food, travel, and fashion.

Love

Meghan used quills and special pens like this one for her calligraphy work.

The Happy Couple

Harry's and Meghan's paths crossed in July 2016, when a mutual friend set them up on a blind date. The couple quickly fell in love and before long, they knew they wanted to spend the rest of their lives together.

Finding time

After only one date, Harry and Meghan immediately wanted to see each other again. It was hard for them to find a time that suited both of their busy schedules, but they managed to see each other at least every two weeks. Sometimes, Meghan flew to the UK to see Harry and other times Harry visited Meghan in Toronto, Canada, where *Suits* was filmed.

∧

For their third date, Harry and Meghan went camping in Botswana, Africa.

Sharing the news

At first, Harry and Meghan tried to keep their relationship private. To stop journalists from seeing them together, they preferred to go on quiet dates out of the public eye. In December 2016, the couple started appearing in public together – shopping for a Christmas tree and attending a play in London.

Popping the question

In November 2017, Harry and Meghan announced the news of their engagement. Harry designed Meghan's engagement ring himself, using diamonds that belonged to his mother. Over Christmas, the Queen marked Meghan's introduction to the family by inviting her to Christmas lunch with Harry's royal relatives.

ROYAL TALK

"The little diamonds on either side are from my mother's jewelry collection, to make sure that she's with us on this crazy journey together."

Harry explained the reason for including his mother's diamonds in Meghan's engagement ring in an interview in 2017.

∧
Harry and Meghan pose for their official engagement photos in November 2017.

Wedding Bells

— • • • —

On May 19, 2018, Harry and Meghan became husband and wife. Their wedding day was traditional but filled with personal touches.

The ceremony

Harry and Meghan's wedding ceremony took place in St. George's Chapel at Windsor Castle. It was attended by around 600 people, including members of the royal family, Meghan's mother and the couple's friends. Meghan's father could not attend for health reasons, so Prince Charles walked her down the aisle.

The Archbishop of Canterbury married Harry and Meghan in a traditional Christian service.
∨

Harry and Meghan walk down the steps of the chapel as husband and wife.

Dressed to impress

Harry and Prince William, his best man, both wore the uniform of Harry's former army regiment. Harry had to get special permission from the Queen to keep his beard for the wedding, as soldiers aren't normally allowed to have beards when in uniform. Meghan wore a simple white dress, designed by the British designer Clare Waight Keller.

Old and new

As is tradition, Harry and Meghan exchanged vows, in which they promised to look after each other. Together with their guests, they sang hymns and the national anthem. Harry and Meghan also put their own twist on the service, with music from a gospel choir.

WEDDING DRESS FUN FACTS

- Meghan wore a tiara that belonged to Harry's great-great-grandmother, Queen Mary.

- Meghan's veil measured 16 feet (5 m) long.

- The veil was embroidered with flowers to represent the 53 Commonwealth countries and California, where Meghan was born.

The Big Day

Harry and Meghan spent the rest of their wedding day celebrating with their friends and family. It was also a day of fun for many people around the world, who hosted parties or watched on TV.

A carriage ride

After the ceremony, Harry and Meghan traveled by carriage through Windsor. They smiled and waved at the thousands of people who filled the streets. This trip was their way of saying thank you to everyone who came to celebrate with them.

∨ People shouted congratulations and waved flags at Harry and Meghan as they rode through the streets of Windsor after their wedding.

Two receptions

At lunchtime, the Queen hosted a reception for the couple and around 600 guests. They enjoyed music from the singer Elton John, who was a close friend of Harry's mother, Diana. In the evening, Prince Charles and Camilla hosted a more relaxed reception for around 200 guests. They enjoyed dinner and dancing, followed by fireworks.

Harry and Meghan drove to the evening reception in a sports car with the license plate E190518 – the date of their wedding! In the UK, dates are written with the day first, followed by the month and year.

A NEW BABY

About a year after the wedding, Harry and Meghan welcomed a son. Born on the morning of May 6, 2019, the child was named Archie Harrison Mountbatten–Windsor. Archie is the seventh in line to the throne, after his father who is sixth in line.

< Meghan and Harry changed clothes before heading to the evening reception.

Helping Others

Harry's mother, Diana, taught her sons about the importance of helping others. Together, they visited homeless shelters and people who were sick with AIDS. These experiences inspired Harry to set up his own charities.

The Royal Foundation

Harry's main charity work is the Royal Foundation, which he set up with William and Kate in 2009. Meghan joined as the fourth patron of the charity in 2017. The charity is made up of many different projects that help to support members of the armed forces and children, and protect endangered animals.

The United for Wildlife project trains wildlife rangers to protect rhinos from hunters who want to kill them for their valuable horns. United for Wildlife is part of the Royal Foundation. ∨

Invictus Games

Harry is well-known for the Invictus Games, a Paralympic-style competition for injured members of the armed forces that he launched in 2014 as part of the Royal Foundation. In the Invictus Games, competitors from around the world take part in different events, including track and field and cycling. Harry believes that sport helps people to recover from their injuries, both physically and mentally. The Invictus Games is also a way of paying respect to those who have served their country.

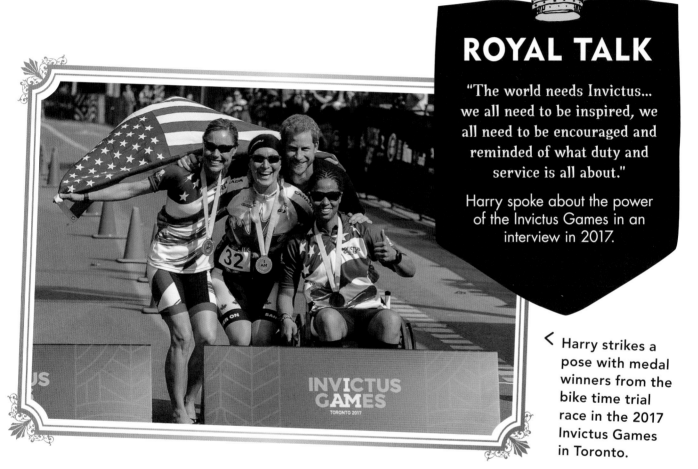

ROYAL TALK

"The world needs Invictus... we all need to be inspired, we all need to be encouraged and reminded of what duty and service is all about."

Harry spoke about the power of the Invictus Games in an interview in 2017.

< Harry strikes a pose with medal winners from the bike time trial race in the 2017 Invictus Games in Toronto.

Mental health

Harry is also passionate about mental health. His campaign Heads Together aims to help people feel more comfortable talking about mental health and get any support that they need. Harry has spoken about how counseling helped him cope after the death of his mother. He hopes that sharing his own experiences with mental health will help people feel less awkward talking about the topic.

Meghan's Charity Work

As a member of the royal family, Meghan is a patron of the Royal Foundation as well as other charities that help people in the UK and Commonwealth. But her charity work started long before she became royal.

Fighting for feminism

Meghan has been passionate about feminism and gender equality since she was a child (see page 11). She has worked with the United Nations to raise awareness of women's issues around the world and the importance of listening to women's views. Meghan has also traveled to other countries, such as India, to better understand the issues that women face there.

‹ Meghan and her mother Doria attend a United Nations event celebrating women in 2015.

ROYAL TALK

"With fame comes opportunity, but in my opinion, it also includes responsibility...to focus less on glass slippers and more on pushing through glass ceilings."

Meghan talks about her responsibility to use her fame to help others in an interview in 2016.

World Vision

From 2016 to 2017, Meghan worked as ambassador for World Vision, the world's largest international children's charity. In her job as ambassador, she made speeches and trips to raise awareness of the work that the charity does. In 2016, she traveled to Rwanda, Africa, with World Vision and met children who had been given access to clean water for the first time, thanks to a new pipeline. Together, they painted watercolor pictures that showed the children's dreams for the future, using clean water from the pipe.

Inspiring others

Meghan has also worked to help the next generation get involved with world issues. As a counselor for the charity One Young World, she joined Harry Potter actor Emma Watson and other celebrities to speak about their charity work. The charity hopes that young people will be inspired by their stories and get involved with their own charity projects.

∨ Meghan had a great time meeting children in Rwanda and learning how clean water benefited their lives.

Hobbies and Interests

Meghan and Harry lead busy lives, in which they have to balance royal responsibilities with their charity work. However, they also make time for different hobbies and interests that bring them joy, such as cooking, sports, and their pets.

Food and cooking

Meghan describes herself as a foodie – someone who loves to cook and eat! Meghan's love of food dates back to her childhood, when she used to pick figs, lemons, and vegetables that she grew in her garden. Today, she still loves to cook with fresh ingredients and make simple dishes such as seafood pasta. However, she also enjoys french fries from time to time! Harry also likes to treat himself from time to time with sticky toffee pudding and cake.

^
Niçoise salad with tuna and egg is one of Meghan's favorite dishes.

Pets

Meghan and Harry are both animal lovers. As a child, Harry had various pets including dogs and ponies. When Meghan moved to the UK, one of her dogs stayed behind with friends in Canada, as the journey would have been too hard for him. However, Meghan was able to bring over her second dog, Guy, who now lives with her and Harry in London. Meghan is passionate about animal adoption and encourages people to rescue animals, rather than buy them.

< Meghan's dog Guy is a beagle, like the dog shown here.

Sports

Harry's childhood love of sports has never gone away. He still enjoys playing sports, such as polo, and watching soccer and rugby matches. He supports the soccer team Arsenal. He also is a big fan of video games, especially the FIFA video games. He played a lot of FIFA while serving in Afghanistan, often beating the other soldiers!

POLO

Polo is a team sport played on horses, in which players have to hit a ball with a long wooden club. It is a popular royal sport — Charles, Harry, and William have all played it, sometimes together on the same team! Harry started to play polo when he was a teenager. Today, he takes part in many charity polo matches with his brother.

Harry takes part in a polo match to support Sentebale, a charity that he founded to help children in Lesotho and Botswana.
∨

Kings and Queens of England

The House of Normandy

William I *(William the Conqueror)*	1066–1087
William II *(William Rufus)*	1087–1100
Henry I	1100–1135
Stephen	1135–1154

The House of Plantagenet

Henry II	1154–1189
Richard I *(Richard the Lionheart)*	1189–1199
John	1199–1216
Henry III	1216–1272
Edward I	1272–1307
Edward II	1307–1327
Edward III	1327–1377
Richard II	1377–1399

The House of Lancaster

Henry IV	1399–1413
Henry V	1413–1422
Henry VI	1422–1461

The House of York

Edward IV	1461–1483
Edward V	1483–1483
Richard III	1483–1485

The House of Tudor

Henry VII	1485–1509
Henry VIII	1509–1547
Edward VI	1547–1553
Jane	1553–1553
Mary I	1553–1558
Elizabeth I	1558–1603

The House of Stuart

James I (James VI of Scotland)	1603–1625
Charles I	1625–1649
Commonwealth declared	
Oliver Cromwell Lord Protector	1653–1658
Richard Cromwell Lord Protector	1658–1659
Monarchy restored	
Charles II	1649 *(restored 1660)*–1685
James II *(James VII of Scotland)*	1685–1688
William III and Mary II	1689–1694 (Mary)
	1689–1702 *(William)*
Anne	1702–1714

The House of Hanover

George I	1714–1727
George II	1727–1760
George III	1760–1820
George IV	1820–1830
William IV	1830–1837
Victoria	1837–1901

The House of Saxe-Coburg – becomes House of Windsor in 1917

Edward VII	1901–1910
George V	1910–1936
Edward VIII *(abdicated)*	1936–1936
George VI	1936–1952
Elizabeth II	1952–

The Royal Family Tree

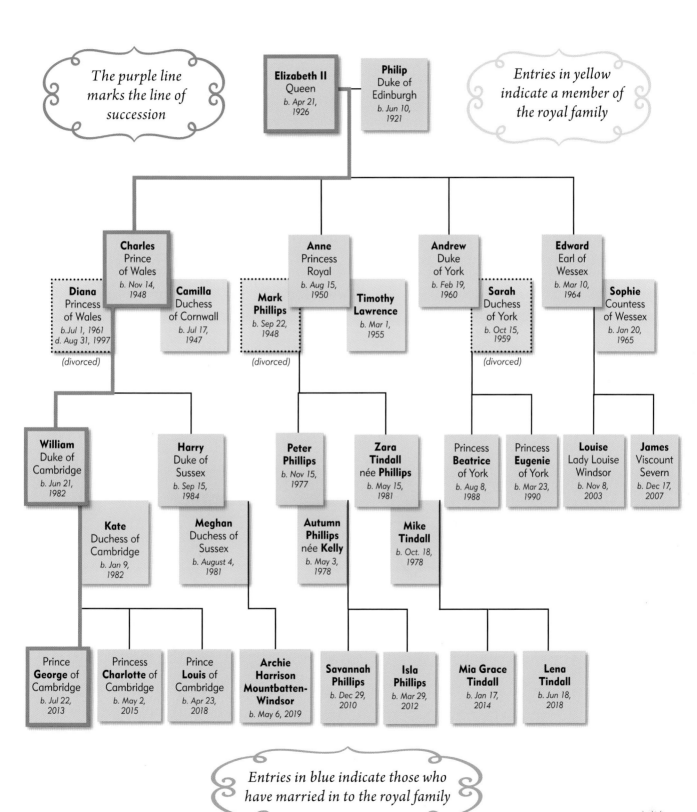

The purple line marks the line of succession

Entries in yellow indicate a member of the royal family

Elizabeth II Queen *b. Apr 21, 1926*

Philip Duke of Edinburgh *b. Jun 10, 1921*

Charles Prince of Wales *b. Nov 14, 1948*

Diana Princess of Wales *b.Jul 1, 1961 d. Aug 31, 1997* (divorced)

Camilla Duchess of Cornwall *b. Jul 17, 1947*

Anne Princess Royal *b. Aug 15, 1950*

Mark Phillips *b. Sep 22, 1948* (divorced)

Timothy Lawrence *b. Mar 1, 1955*

Andrew Duke of York *b. Feb 19, 1960*

Sarah Duchess of York *b. Oct 15, 1959* (divorced)

Edward Earl of Wessex *b. Mar 10, 1964*

Sophie Countess of Wessex *b. Jan 20, 1965*

William Duke of Cambridge *b. Jun 21, 1982*

Kate Duchess of Cambridge *b. Jan 9, 1982*

Harry Duke of Sussex *b. Sep 15, 1984*

Meghan Duchess of Sussex *b. August 4, 1981*

Peter Phillips *b. Nov 15, 1977*

Autumn Phillips née **Kelly** *b. May 3, 1978*

Zara Tindall née **Phillips** *b. May 15, 1981*

Mike Tindall *b. Oct. 18, 1978*

Princess **Beatrice** of York *b. Aug 8, 1988*

Princess **Eugenie** of York *b. Mar 23, 1990*

Louise Lady Louise Windsor *b. Nov 8, 2003*

James Viscount Severn *b. Dec 17, 2007*

Prince **George** of Cambridge *b. Jul 22, 2013*

Princess **Charlotte** of Cambridge *b. May 2, 2015*

Prince **Louis** of Cambridge *b. Apr 23, 2018*

Archie Harrison Mountbatten-Windsor *b. May 6, 2019*

Savannah Phillips *b. Dec 29, 2010*

Isla Phillips *b. Mar 29, 2012*

Mia Grace Tindall *b. Jan 17, 2014*

Lena Tindall *b. Jun 18, 2018*

Entries in blue indicate those who have married in to the royal family

29

Glossary

active service fighting in a war zone

ambassador someone who represents something, such as their country

calligrapher someone who does beautiful handwriting

dormitory a shared room with multiple beds

gap year a year between finishing school and starting university or training in which people travel or work

graduate to complete a degree at a university or other school

patron a person who supports an organization or charity

polo a sport played on horseback in which players hit a ball with long wooden hammers

represent to act on behalf of someone or many people. Prince Harry represents the UK when he attends events and meetings with leaders from other countries.

sexist suggesting that one gender is not as good as another

the Commonwealth a group of countries, including the UK, that were previously part of the British Empire and share trade agreements

Trooping the Colour a celebration held each year to mark the Queen's birthday

Further Information

Books:

Bailey, Jacqui. *Queen Elizabeth II's Britain*. London, England: Franklin Watts, 2015.

Gagne, Tammy. *Prince Harry*. Hallandale, FL: Mitchell Lane Publishers, 2019.

Gogerly, Liz. *A Royal Childhood: 200 Years of Royal Babies*. London, England: Franklin Watts, 2017.

Manning, Mike, and Brita Granström. *The Story of Britain*. London, England: Franklin Watts, 2016.

Websites:

Harry's official website has lots of information about his life and charity work: ***www.royal.uk/prince-harry***

Visit the website of the Royal Foundation to find out more about the different projects that they support: ***www.royalfoundation.com***

The official website of the royal family has details of all its members, as well as royal residences and events such as Trooping the Colour: ***www.royal.uk/royal-family***

Publisher's note to educators and parents: Our editors have carefully reviewed these websites to ensure that they are suitable for students. Many websites change frequently, however, and we cannot guarantee that a site's future contents will continue to meet our high standards of quality and educational value. Be advised that students should be closely supervised whenever they access the Internet.

Index